Pokemon Go: Diary Of A Wimpy Pikachu 2: Pokemon Go Adventure

This book is Part 2 of the Diary of A Wimpy Pikachu series

To avoid any spoilers, please read this book first...

Diary of A Wimpy Pikachu 1 ➜ *http://amzn.to/2b0BfSC*

WEDNESDAY

We left Kanto yesterday.

There are a bunch of us now. Misty and her team of pokemon invited us to travel with her and we got on the boat yesterday night. Me and the other non-water pokemon have been having a hard time getting used to the whole floating on water thing. I got sick twice this morning, alone. There is just so much rocking! But Ash told me and the others that we may not have to be out in the water too long – only a few days, hopefully. He's also trying to take the opportunity to catch a few water pokemon.

I have been mostly sleeping.

2

FRIDAY

Ash caught a Staryu and told me that we will be on land tomorrow.

I don't even know where we're going, but when we get there, I am kissing the ground! Everyone seems to have gotten used to this horrible trip except Zubat and me. He's a wreck. Last night, I found him curled up below deck, mumbling something about sea monsters and echolocation... All I could do was sit there and console him as best as I could. While we were talking, though, I heard an uproar of exclamations from above. I checked in with Zubat one more time, throwing him a reassuring smile, and then I bolted upstairs.

Misty was on her toes, leaned over the railing of the boat. I only did that when I had to hurl. I scurried over to her, patting the back of her leg.

"Pika?" I whispered, trying to help. She didn't move, but shot a response back at me from over the railing.

"No, Pikachu! Look out into the water!!"

I looked around the main deck, seeing Ash and all of the others doing what Misty was, including the audible oooooo's and awwwww's. As much as the moving waves nauseated me, I leaped into the air and caught hold of the ledge. I felt Misty's hands steadying me as I almost tottered over. After gaining my balance and peering out like everyone else, I could see what they were so amazed at.

A beautiful array of red light was around us. The water glowed in blinking pink and ruby, even the side of the boat showing off the light. Misty saw the confused amazement on my face and grinned. "They're Staryus. Cool, right?"

Staryu

Cool was an understatement. Just then, I saw a flash of

light and heard cheers from the other side of the deck. I turned to see Ash clutching tightly to a pokeball and beaming with accomplishment. He had caught one of them. Ash was getting better at identifying and catching pokemon. I flashed back to the first water pokemon that he'd caught, Krabby, and the very little time that I'd spent with him before he ran off. I looked back over the ledge, staring at the pretty symphony of blinking lights and deciding that this trip was going to be great. Had this happened every night? Had I been missing out on all of this when I was sleeping or sulking?

I ran over to Ash for a congratulatory hug. He hugged me back.

"I'm so excited, Pikachu. We are hitting land tomorrow."

5

SATURDAY

LAND. FINALLY.

We reached land today and I could not be happier.

All of us have been walking all day, though, and I don't think that Ash and Misty know where to go.

SUNDAY

We spent the day at camp and Misty got into a battle.

Let me tell you what happened. Okay, so, after walking for a day and a half, Ash finally decided we should make camp. The region we are in seems rockier than the forests that I am used to, and the ground is very dusty and sandy where it meets the water. But we are now in a wooded area near a place that Ash and Misty call Goldenrod City. Misty left earlier today to check it out and see if she could trade for some supplies. But instead, she came running back to camp in a panic. Ash got to her first.

"Misty! What happened to--"

But before he could finish his question, she pushed past him, grabbing at a few of her pokeballs. The ones she grabbed, I didn't recognize. I knew immediately what was happening. She looked behind her and a familiar guy appeared.

"Look, Brock, I told you that the next time we ran into each other, we would battle. I am tired of you telling me that I can't be a great trainer because I'm a girl. It's ridiculous!"

The boy she called Brock laughed.

"And what are the chances that we would land in Johto at the same time?! I am going to love beating you and taking whatever baby pokemon you have."

Misty moved toward the center of camp and tossed a pokeball into the air, letting it burst open and, after a flash of light, a large blue and brown mass emerged. At the same time, Brock summoned an Onix and the ground shook as it barreled over to us. Ash and I backed up. Misty didn't seem to want any outside help. I looked over at Misty, and beside her stood a Wartortle. He looked over at me and chuckled. Just then, he jumped into action, dodging what seemed to be a surprise attack, hopping to the side, and rolling into his shell. Onix burrowed straight into a tree. As he arose from the hole in the ground, Misty kicked a huge bucket of water toward Wartortle and he sucked it up, then sprayed it directly into Onix's face.

Onix hit the tree again, this time from the force of the water attack. I couldn't help but cheer. Brock dashed to his pokemon's side, turning to shoot a scorned look at Misty. Wartortle stood tall. He'd won with almost no work at all. Misty squealed with delight and Ash shouted cheers and praise.

"This isn't fair! He's evolved! You chose an evolved pokemon to battle!"

Wartortle
Vs.
Onix

Brock was devastated, but no one was paying him any mind. Misty walked away, patting her Wartortle on his head and giggling to herself. Ash turned to Brock.

"I think it's time for you to go."

Wartortle chittered at Misty's praise and treats, and I walked over, too.

This was the best introduction to a new friend.

10

TUESDAY

This whole Pokemon GO thing is insane.

Ash and Misty have made friends with a bunch of local
trainers that use it. I don't like the way they look at Ash and
Misty, though. They admire them, saying they are original
trainers, but they use their little computer things to do
everything. This Pokemon GO system tracks pokemon for
you and even supplies you with a tracker for poke stops.
But the worst part is that me and the rest of Ash and Misty's
pokemon can't go too far away from camp without the
other trainers trying to catch us. Especially me.

I really don't know why, either! I'm just a wimpy little
Pikachu. But, for some reason, they are obsessed with
catching one. I am the only Pikachu I know of personally,
but I also know that there are more of us around. Maybe
not here in Johto, but they are around. Anyway, I'm tired of
it. Ash has been pretending like it's not happening. I can't
even go 30 feet from camp, though, without running into
some crazed Pokemon GO trainers trying to nab me. Brock
has even started hanging out with us to get away from
them. Onix isn't so bad either. He's really quiet, but likes to
keep watch for us while we go out to get food. He saved me
yesterday, actually.

Eevee and I were on our way to this decent-sized apple tree behind our camp when a kid ran out in front of us. He was laughing, and pointed directly at me.

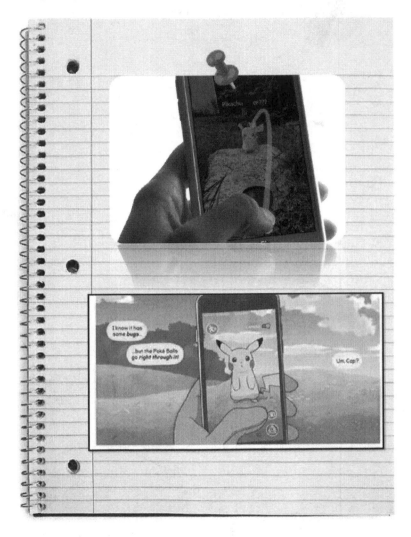

"OH MY GOD! A Pikachu! I have been tracking you for hours! It said you were nearby, but you just walked right up to me!"

12

It took a second more, but then he started throwing pokeballs. I dodged, but I knew it was only a matter of time before I was caught. Eevee had bolted as soon as he'd noticed the guy. I didn't blame him. Suddenly, Onix appeared. He was able to be stealthy because of his underground digging thing. He rumbled up and grabbed my foot in his rocky mouth. I fell to the ground with a thud – and it hurt pretty badly, but it was better than getting caught by some weirdo. Onix dragged me home in silence and dropped me right in front of camp.

"Thanks, Onix," I mumbled as he somberly rolled away.

In all the time I have been spending on trying to get away from these people, I haven't really gotten the opportunity to get to know the new guy. Misty keeps Wartortle close to home and Ash is always sending me to get supplies. Misty is scared that Wartortle will run away or get poached by the crazy Pokemon GO trainers, but I think he can hold his own.

Other than the new trainers, life has been super slow. My training has slowed down because Misty and Ash seem to still be trying to figure out where we're going next. I think Brock may even be coming with us. I already hate it here, and we've only been in Johto for a week or so.

WEDNESDAY

Last night, Misty convinced Brock and Ash that it's time to leave camp.

"We gotta get out of here. Our pokemon are no good here without getting any training or any decent battling. We've been here for a solid week and a half, and have not accomplished anything."

I looked over and saw Brock twitch, probably remembering his very recent butt whooping. I have been ready to go for days now. This whole Pokemon GO thing has everyone out of sorts, and training just hasn't been the focus. I've thought about leaving on my own, too, it's been so bad. Ash seems to have lost some of his fire for seeing what's going on in the training world outside of Kanto. It's so different from home, and he's having trouble adjusting. But the saddest part of it all is how little he seems to care that his team is unhappy. I miss my freedom and he just mopes.

14

FRIDAY

We leave today.

I know that Pokemon GO training exists all over the place, but at least by leaving we have a chance to build the team. Ash agreed to leave, finally – half-heartedly, but at least he's agreed. We packed everything up yesterday and Zubat had to practically drag Ash to his feet this morning. We all pitched in on gathering rations and Misty went into town with Brock to trade for some other supplies. When they came back, we pushed off.

We had to walk in a weird pyramid formation to keep everyone together, but we figured out a system where all of the team's pokemon are safe. I had to smash between Wartortle and Onix. They laughed when they heard they were protecting me, especially Wartortle.

16

"But he's so small! And WIMPY!!"

Him and Onix burst into laughter, which was the first time I had ever heard something so loud come out of Onix's mouth.

They were right, too, but something about me was important. Too bad I didn't even know what it was. I could see the trainers, too, trailing us in the woods. If I learned anything growing up as a small and wimpy pokemon, it was to watch out for your surroundings. But they looked like they were tracking something ahead of us. I sped up a little bit. Maybe it was a super rare pokemon or something even better...

I caught up to Misty, Brock, and Ash, who was still sulking a bit, but standing up straight for a change. They'd noticed it, too. Each of them had a pokedex out. Misty mumbled something about the "region" and Brock grunted in response. They were tracking something. I moved back to my place between Wartortle and Onix. There was something special about me. I had to sandwich myself in for protection from a bunch of crazed kids, between an evolved fighting machine and a rock snake. This was probably the coolest thing that would ever happen to me. We seemed to have forsaken our "get out of here" plan for something big, but I still didn't know that it was.

But, I really hope that we find out soon.

SUNDAY

I've gotten used to this whole boat thing now.

We boarded yesterday.

Brock calls himself "an expert traveler," but Misty and Ash just laugh every time he says it. We should be on the boat for another few days.

19

Thursday

It's been a while since I last wrote.

But, it's just been so nice. We are all together and happy again, without having other trainers and battles to worry about. The only thing is, Ash has been talking about going into Pokemon GO training. Him and Misty got into an argument yesterday.

"---can't you see we are behind? The way we train is old, and they laugh at us because we aren't updated!"

He'd finally opened up to Misty and I yesterday, and had been going on about it for most of the trip. He's determined to convince us all that he's right. Misty isn't having it.

"Ash, you can't let them get to you! We are great trainers! We can go to gyms – HECK, Brock used to run one! And they don't know half of what we do about pokemon. When I met you, I knew that your passion would make you an amazing trainer, and it has!"

I stepped forward.

I've been thinking about why I stay with Ash a lot lately. He's so young, and sometimes just as childish as me. I think most of the time that I am just as wise as he is, give or take some situations. We seem to just fit together. He understands me. Pokemon GO has made training a thing that anyone can do, and some of them are probably really good, but Ash is better than really good. I went into battle for him before I even really knew him. And that was before I was properly being trained or before I had ever even been in a real fight.

I smiled at him, being swayed by the moving waves. If this had been almost a month ago, I would have been puking my brains out right now. He looked at me; the frustration in his gaze was slowly melting away.

"We're a good team. You know that. Remember what the professor said."

He laughed as he always did when I said something he considered profound. Misty laughed, too, appearing to be happy that tensions were broken. Ash turned to Misty again.

"Pikachu was my first catch. He defended me in my first battle with almost no training. He's facing his fears at the same time as I am. You're right – there is something special about being a trainer that I am finding with each of my pokemon, and those trainers are missing out."

I was still super wimpy, and so was Ash and a good portion of our team, too. But we were a family. Even Brock, after getting beaten (pretty badly) by Misty, had seen it and stayed with us. This was about more that just "catching 'em all" as Ash used to put it. It's about loving what you do, and that's most important.

I am excited to go back to being a team and showing these other trainers who's boss.

SATURDAY

We got to Hoenn today.

When we got off of the boat, Ash told me that the first stop we were making was at a gym.

I have never been to a pokemon gym before and Ash keeps telling me that I will like this one. The whole group of us passed through a city called Slateport. Misty ran into the market and traded some berries she'd picked in Johto for some vitamins and things. We then went and made camp in a clearing we came across in the woods. As Misty, Brock, and the other pokemon went to work, some other Pokemon GO trainers were there packing up their things. Ash stepped up first, reaching a hand out to shake.

"Hey, guys! What's up? We just got here and we're hoping to set up camp here. Have you been here long?"

There were two trainers standing in front of us. A guy and a girl, both a little older than Ash. They each took turns shaking his hand.

"Yeah, we're, uhhh, headed out now."

The guy was looking past Ash, at me, standing a few feet behind him. The girl was busy swiping around on her handheld device now, not really paying attention to Ash.

"Cool! We're actually headed to this gym in a city near here; have you heard anything about a guy named

Wattson?"

The girl sighed and looked at Ash with narrowed eyes.

"Uhhhhh, that guy is in Mauville City. It's close. We don't really train in those gyms anymore, though, so I don't know much else."

She then turned toward the guy she was with, who was still looking at me, and made an impatient face. He must have seen her out of the corner of his eye.

"Alright, man! I wish you and your Pikachu well, and hope you catch 'em all! Good luck!"

Ash curtly nodded and swiftly turned back to me. They disappeared into the brush nearby. "We are going to see that trainer! Hopefully, he can teach you a thing or two in battle because he's a specialist in electric-type pokemon. We gotta make you stronger, Pika."

Suddenly, I was really excited. I wasn't much for combat, but the idea of a trainer that was an expert in my type was so cool! I grinned in response. My skills were becoming really important to me. I jumped for joy and somewhere in the air lost my footing, landing flat on my face. Ash rushed to help me up, but I heard a symphony of laughter from behind me. After getting back on my feet, I turned around to see Butterfree, Eevee, and Zubat, all in a full roaring fit. They had joined the rest of the pokemon in poking fun. It didn't bother me. As a matter of fact, I also found it funny. I giggled to myself and approached the group.

"So, you're gonna train in a gym, huh?" Wartortle boomed

from behind me. I nodded with a little more enthusiasm than I felt.

"That's cool, man. I think you could really benefit from that."

I smiled and nodded, and he laughed again, ruffling the top of my head and then thundering off to sit with Onix for dinner.

SUNDAY

We are going to the electric-type pokemon trainer tomorrow and I couldn't be more ecstatic.

Some of the other pokemon are jealous, but Onix defended me by saying I was weak and that my abilities were "too important of an asset to not strengthen." After the initial shock of him stringing such a profound statement together, they reluctantly all agreed. The few times when I have gotten into a situation that required me to defend myself, I've mostly lost. There were some really scary pokemon that hung around when I was growing up. The whole "self-defense" thing just didn't seem like something I was capable of. I know now that I can do it, but I just need to train better.

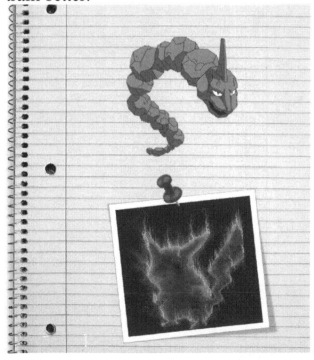

MONDAY

...I trained with Wattson today.

Okay, so, I got to train with a professional and embarrassed myself. It was only the first day, at least – that's what I am telling myself.

Ash took me into Mauville City to the gym to meet Wattson. On the way, we had to ask a few Pokemon GO trainers for directions even though the city was pretty close. They barely looked up from their mobile devices to direct us. A couple of guys just pointed in a general direction and kept walking. We finally got there this morning. Ash knocked on the door and loud, padding footsteps approached from the other side. The door suddenly swung open and a very large man was standing in front of us. I jumped and fell on my back. His laughter boomed.

"HELLOOOOO!! I'm guessing that you are Ash? And that must mean that this little guy is your Pikachu. Hey, friend!"

He squatted down in front of me and put a hand out. I grabbed it, even though I could feel a few nervous sparks of static at my fingertips. He yelped, pulling his hand back. He shook it and let out a long whistle then. "Well, you are definitely in the right place! COME ON IN!"

Ash and I walked into the gym and saw that no one was inside but us. Wattson turned to us.

"Yeah, I was super excited to hear from you because my gym hasn't been getting much business. This Pokemon GO craze has really taken older gyms off of the map because these trainers are running their own gyms."

I looked around and felt a little sad. I scurried over to what looked like the main floor and waited. I was ready to learn. Wattson barreled over with a pokeball in hand. A beam of light shot out and a small metal ball rolled out. It stopped in the air and I realized that it was a Magnemite. He squealed, hovering across the floor from me. I relaxed, and suddenly the ground shook and rumbled. Magnemite was on the move. He zoomed up to me and, before I could react, I was frozen in place. His magnets vibrated and one of the steel beams nearby lifted off of the ground and barreled toward us.

I flinched, breaking free of the thunder wave hold I was in. But instead of attacking, I ran.

Wattson

WEDNESDAY

ALRIGHT.

So, the beginning of my training was a little rough. Ash told me it was okay, but I realized on Monday that this training thing is going to take a little more work than I anticipated. I can't help but wonder why there are still physical gyms. I know that Pokemon GO allows there to be "virtual" training (whatever that is), and that sounds so much easier than coming to see Wattson three times a week. The trainers that Ash and I run into on the way to the gym are placing bets on how long it takes us to "come to the darkside" (no idea what that means either), though, and it's really irritating me. I like Wattson and Magnemite; I've gotten to know both of them in the last few days and they are great! Magnemite is super dorky and Wattson is just always making jokes. I like being able to see them and benefit from their experience. But I can't help feeling like maybe it would be a lot easier to do the Pokemon GO thing.

Ash doesn't know, but I made friends with one of the GO trainers that lives close to the outskirts of the city. Ash had me go to training on my own yesterday. He and Brock had to take care of something and it conflicted with my training time. So, on my walk, I crossed paths with an abnormally normal and polite Pokemon GO trainer. He said that he already had a Pikachu, so it didn't really interest him that I was walking around alone. I'd had to evade a couple of trainers before him, though. He asked me where I was headed and, in my hesitation to tell him, he told me that he was training one of his Eevees as we were speaking. That interested me. So, he showed me the little device he was using, and the screen actually showed the inside of a gym. A very small version of one, but it was a gym. It was so strange. He also was doing all of it on his own!

"...See? And I just work on developing their combat power and different moves! You can dodge by doing this! Can you---"

I jumped up. I was super late. I ran straight to the gym to meet Wattson. I hadn't even caught the trainer's name.

All during my training with Magnemite, I wanted to ask him if he had seen virtual gyms like I saw with that kid. I knew that he had been doing this for a while and that his brother, Magneton, was even more experienced. I wasn't ready to spar with him yet. But, I wanted to know what he thought about it. Wattson was around to supervise the training the whole time, though, and so I had no time to talk to him in private.

Was it wrong for me to think this new way was useful? Ash was taking so much time to take me to the gym when he had other pokemon to care for and other responsibilities to tend to. Maybe I could learn how to do it and teach Ash?

FRIDAY

I don't think I will ever be done training.

EVER.

First of all, I ran into that trainer kid again. The one Pokemon GO trainer I have ever "hung out" with. He stopped by the camp to see Misty about some berries for trade in the cities. I had no idea that Misty even interacted with anyone but us and the people in the surrounding cities. As soon as I saw him, I ran to hide. I never talked to Ash about the whole virtual training thing because I knew what he would say. He really liked being able to take me to a professional trainer like the professor told him about. Brock is also a trainer, and used to run a gym of his own, so he's morally against Pokemon GO training and preaches against it almost daily.

I was hiding in a small patch of shrubs by Misty's tent when Togepi waddled over. I tried to wave him away, but he wasn't taking a hint. After about 20 minutes of Togepi sitting beside my hiding place, the kid finally left after his meeting with Misty. I have training tomorrow and, at this point, I'm really tired of going. It has been a WEEK, but it feels like it's been a month. Yesterday, Magnemite complimented me on my improvement, but then Wattson told me if I didn't show more improvement that I would have to train for a lot longer.

SATURDAY

I am just thinking a lot.

Since we have been here for a little while, I have gotten pretty comfortable with roaming the area alone. At this point, Ash does not take me to the gym. Though he should be. Half of training is bonding with your trainer and getting "in sync for battle." I miss the easier times, though. I just liked being around the group and going on hunts with Ash in the beginning, and now it just feels like I am on my own most of the time. And it doesn't help when Pokemon GO exists and I have to cower in the bushes when I see a crazed player. I don't think about Pokemon GO as an option for the crew anymore.

This isn't because it's not a good option – it's just not our option. You can't even walk with your fellow pokemon! After me, Ash has been pretty good about letting his new pokemon stretch their legs and even choose if they want to leave. There are some that can't really function in the wild and need to be kept in pokeballs, like little bug types or some more dangerous and poisonous ones. But I am just really missing being a poke family. I wonder what it is like, being a team in Pokemon GO? Magnemite told me that they don't get to talk to each other. By they, he meant the other pokemon.

"Yeah, they just exist in isolation, but with the same trainer! It's inhumane!"

I laughed, but a part of me believed him. What does that mean for them, though, and could they be freed? Those are the two questions that keep playing over and over again in my head.

Monday

Since I found out the truth, I have gone back to avoiding Pokemon GO trainers altogether.

Onix and I have gotten to know each other really well over these past few weeks, too. Dude, he's a really great conversationalist.

"I'm hoping we pick up and find camp somewhere new soon. We haven't seen any real action out here, and Brock is tired of just giving advice and helping train other rock-types in town."

Oh yeah, I forgot to say that Brock has become a bit of a small city celebrity. The traditional trainers here all love him because he still physically trains rock-types. They knew his name from back home and, after a whole lot of begging, they finally got him to hold open sessions about 3 times a week. It's been great for us because they pay him in food and other gear, but according to Onix, he's bored. He left home to be a trainer with his own pokemon to train, and yet here he was, back to being a gym master.

- THESE DONUTS ARE GREAT!
JELLY-FILLED ARE MY FAVORITE.

I spoke up. "Yeah, I am also hoping to scoot soon. I feel like I'm hitting a wall in training and Wattson is starting to creep me out."

He really was. The smiling all the time just really made me feel uneasy. He laughed the other day when one of those pillars hit me and I can still hear it echo in my nightmares.

"I'm also really tired of seeing the same GO trainers. They're harmless at this point because they all know us, but ever since Magnemite told me they just trap and store their pokemon in complete isolation, I've been terrified."

I let off a little shiver for effect. Onix sat up and cocked his head to the side.

"Wait, you mean the pokemon can't talk to each other or hang out?!! What kind of team is that?! That's wild and super not cool!!!"

Onix was reaching full-blown hysterics, and although it alarmed me, it was comforting. I didn't know what to do about the situation other than for us to plant ourselves in a new spot on the island and hope that I didn't have to talk to another GO trainer again. It was very unlikely, but a nice thought.

Onix was still standing on his tail and flailing in distress, which was now kind of hilarious. I choked back laughter and approached him as he rolled backward in disbelief.

"Onix, it's okay. I'm actually trying to figure out a way to free them. Magnemite also told me that trainers pick their favorite to train the most and use them to take over virtual gyms."

I mean, that isn't much different from traditional training, but at least the other pokemon aren't neglected, in our way of training. The thought of it just made me cringe. Onix at some point had calmed down and moved closer to me in a sitting position.

"I am hoping that we can figure out a way to stop--"

Onix squinted at me and I knew immediately what he was thinking. He leaned in and whispered, "What would happen if you got caught and tried to get out?"

Tuesday

Now that we had come up with this RIDICULOUS idea, we needed a plan.

Onix and I decided that it would have to be me. I would have to get caught, and then find my way out of the game. I don't exactly know how we got to that conclusion, but I am on board. The next few days, we are going to have to dedicate to planning.

THURSDAY

After bringing the other team pokemon onboard, we have decided to set the plan in motion this Saturday. I am hoping that it works, but the plan looks a little like this:

1. I have to make myself visible. Onix told me about a spot that Brock is always complaining about where Pokemon GO trainers hang out. It's something called a pokestop. It's really close to the gym, so I can find my way there.

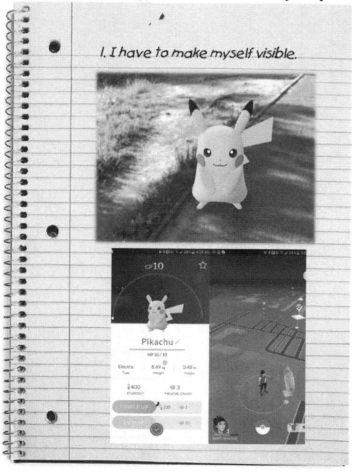

2. I obviously have to get myself caught. But just so I am not going in without some kind of security blanket on the outside, Wartortle and Eevee are going to keep watch from close by. Just so they can see who is catching me and keep an eye on them for however long I will be in.

3. I have to figure out an exit point. This is going to be the hard part and may take some time. I also don't know how long it's going to take before I get stuck or something, too.

I have not told any of the trainers and do not plan to. The only pokemon among us who seem to be iffy on that part are Togepi and Butterfree.

But Wartortle and Onix seem to scare them enough to have convinced them not to tell anyone. But I can't pretend like I'm not just as wimpy as they are. I am super nervous this will not work. I am going in there alone and, even with all of my training, I have no idea what I am walking into. I had no idea what technology was until Ash introduced me to the pokedex, and that's apparently obsolete now? Oh God. What am I doing? Why wouldn't one of the bigger evolved pokemon do this?! They make fun of me for being small and cowardly, and then make me do something totally stupid!

FRIDAY

I am going in tomorrow and I couldn't be more nervous.

All of the other pokemon keep giving me these pitiful looks like I'm marching to my death or something. They aren't helping. Tomorrow, I am going to leave camp like I am going to training and set the plan into motion. Of all the pokemon in our cohort, the only one to give me a legitimate pep talk was Wartortle. He caught me right before dinner and pulled me aside to talk.

"Look, man, what you are doing is probably one of the bravest but DUMBEST things I have ever heard of. But you are doing it for the right reasons and we are going to be there on the sidelines waiting for you to hop right back out."

I really hope he's right. Otherwise, who knows what will happen?

SATURDAY

Togepi told on me.

I have very little patience for tattle tales, and Togepi wimped out at the last second and told Misty what we were planning. Ash was made aware shortly after returning to camp last night. Misty made me wait in Ash's tent for him.

"WHAT ARE YOU THINKING?! Are you trying to get away from me or the team?! Is it training? – I-I don't even know what would make you want to get caught by some random Pokemon GO trainer! You are just beginning professional training, and you are very small and inexperienced, Pikachu!"

His voice had been softening toward the end. Usually, when Ash was angry about something, it was just easier for everyone to let him explode and fizzle out. I waited for him to tire out and then he sat down, waiting for me to explain myself.

"Pika."

I sighed and patted his arm.

"I want to help other pokemon. It is part of why I choose to be with you as a trainer. I love being on your team, but something about virtual training makes me feel like it is wrong. Other pokemon have ideas of what it is like and the idea is scary! We want to help them. This is the only way we thought we could."

I didn't think I had ever said this much to Ash before – not at one time. It felt good to explain myself.

"Pikachu, I know what you are trying to accomplish, but I

cannot let you put yourself at risk like this. You are not ready for such a mission! I am still training you for basic combat!"

This was making me angry now.

"YOU are not training me anymore, Ash. You are my trainer, but you send me to a gym that I have grown to hate. I wish you would spend more time with me like before, but all you do is run around with Misty and Brock. You are too busy to even hang out with me! I HAVE to do this. I can't just sit around and not try SOMETHING."

I somehow knew that the other pokemon in our camp were listening outside and silently cheering me on. This did not normally happen. Pokemon did not argue with their trainers, but Ash had always treated me like a peer. We were friends.

"I – I don't know..."

Ash was stroking his chin now. I could tell he was thinking. Suddenly, he stood up and left the tent. I quickly followed him out and found him standing in the middle of the camp.

"I want to help them, too."

He turned to me and smiled sadly.

"Even if it means possibly losing you."

I scurried closer to him. He knew what was at stake here, but I did, too, and he was respecting that. I was going to miss that if things did not go as planned. I didn't know why

I'd ever tried to hide it from him. Pokemon GO trainers could never have this kind of relationship with their pokemon, and that was wrong. The new plan was going to be set in motion on Monday.

SUNDAY

There is a new, slightly different plan in motion.

The trainers wanted to be included and Ash came up with a few changes.

1. I will still be approaching the "pokestop" we intended, but I will be going at a less busy time. More experienced trainers hang out there on the off hours, and the more professional the Pokemon GO trainer, the better (according to Ash and Brock).

2. Ash wanted to make sure that I had a way of communicating with him when I get in there. So, he rigged a pokedex for two-way walkie talkie communication and I am supposed to smuggle it in there with me. He says that it should work for a few days, but not long with the other "electronic interference." Whatever that means...

3. Misty and Brock are going to track the trainer who catches me. Misty said that she will even befriend them, just so they are close and can't head off of the island or anything. They are also going to do some research themselves on the outside.

4. I cannot go alone. A huge change in the plan is that I have to take someone with me. But that's the tricky part – we don't know if I will be caught by the same trainer as whoever goes with me. I am still working on getting Ash to change his mind, but he is sure that I am more likely to get out if I find someone to take with me.

I don't know if I am ready. But, Eevee volunteered yesterday to go with me. We leave tomorrow night.

MONDAY

The night time in the woods is always scary away from camp. It's even scarier when you are marching into a very stupid plan.

Eevee and I said goodbye to the rest of the gang, getting sage battle advice and a few tears from our peers. Togepi apologized for tattling and gave me a hug. He was forgiven immediately. I am not good at holding grudges, especially when it's possible I will never see him again. Ash refused to say goodbye, or even "Bon Voyage" like Brock did. He was determined to keep his emotions out of this and I was going to try to respect that.

"You ready to go?" he grunted, curtly. He handed me my radio, which I had decided to tape to my side under my arm. Just for safekeeping. He didn't look me in my eyes like he did normally, and I knew that he was nervous.

"Pika."

I held my eyes on the back of his bobbing head as he fiddled with his radio-dex. He'd convinced Misty to lend him hers so that I had a way of talking to him with mine.

"I don't want Eevee to go."

He perked up, about to protest, and then caught himself.

"Okay."

I knew that was really bothering him, too, but I did not care. I was going to do this on my own. No one else was getting trapped if things went wrong. Eevee seemed to melt at the news. The initial bravery was appreciated, but unnecessary.

I let out a deep breath, and marched with Misty, Ash, and Brock out of camp. Silence fell as we left.

Thank you for reading *Diary Of A wimpy Pikachu 2: Pokemon Adventure*. I hope you enjoyed it! If you did…

1. Help other people find this by writing a review

➔ *http://amzn.to/2ctL4XR*

2. Sign up for my new releases e-mail, so you can find out about the next book as soon as it's available

➔ *http://smarturl.it/PokemonGuide*

3. Follow me at Amazon

➔ *https://www.amazon.com/Red-Smith/e/B01LCO1066*

4. Which Pokémon do you want to meet? Comment in the review and I will get your favorite Pokémon's Diary out soon!

➔ *http://amzn.to/2ctL4XR*

Keep reading for a preview of _Diary Of A Wimpy Pikachu 3: Pokemon Escapee_, it's available now!

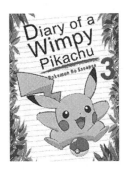

Diary of a Wimpy Pikachu 3 ➜ http://amzn.to/2eG4Fnz

TUESDAY

I got caught today.

Although this was intentional, it was also just as terrifying as the first time. Actually, this time might have been more terrifying.

So a big part of being caught by a Pokemon GO trainer is the process of actually getting sucked into the game. There is still that flash of light like with a regular Pokeball but your body is miniaturized and absorbed into the little device instead. It kind of hurts. Ash and the gang were behind me the whole time and I heard Misty gasp when I was pulled in. I didn't even see the trainer's face but I heard a girl's voice cheer when the light shot off.

Everything was dark around me at first. Almost as if I was sitting in a sea of blackness. I have never experienced this kind of darkness before. I tried to spark a little light from my paws but I was shaking too much to get it to work. There was also a humming. Ash had warned me about this. He said that electricity often has a sound. It surrounded me like a swarm of beedrills. It made my skin vibrate. There was suddenly a huge flash of white and I was standing in what felt like a glass box. I looked around immediately.

Around me, there were a bunch of other boxes. All labelled and filled with Pokemon. On the labels I could see, there were things like names of the Pokemon, weight, type and height. There were also other things I couldn't quite read from where I was standing. Some of the boxes also had gold stars on them. I looked up to see that mine did too. What does that even mean? In the glass box beside me was what appeared to be a Gastly. It had the same menacing face it always did and bobbed mindlessly in its cage. On my left there was a resting Growlithe. Both of them also had stars.

I turned to the Growlithe and tapped on my side of the cage.

"PIKA?!"

My neighbour, *Growlithe*

It didn't seem to hear me. I tapped again, this time flailing my arms immediately afterward, hoping that sudden movement would stir a response. Nothing happened. I suddenly got an idea. I remembered a move that Wattson had taught me, where I jump and create a sudden burst of light. I could only get it to work about once a session because I wasn't strong enough to control it yet. I steadied myself in the middle of the cage and closed my eyes. All at once, I dove for the side of the cage and shot as much light as I could from my tail in the air. Although my eyes were closed and I couldn't see what was happening, I could feel the heat coming off of me.

When I landed, there was a moment before I could lift my head to look up. I took a second and looked over my paws, laid out on front of me. The Growlithe was looking right at me and smiling.

After I got his attention, Growlithe just stared at me for awhile.

He seemed to be trying to figure out how to respond to me since no sound seemed to escape the cages. He placed his paws on the side facing me; stretching and let them fall again.

I have to figure out how to talk to him.

Other Awesome Books by the Author

Gotta Grab'em All

Diary of a Pokemon Trainer 1

Download Here: <u>*http://amzn.to/2bHzR7q*</u>

Diary of a Pokemon Trainer 2

Download Here: <u>http://amzn.to/2eoosGq</u>

Diary of a Pokemon Trainer 3 ➔
http://amzn.to/2eZq9xG

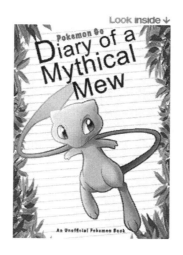

Diary of a Mythical Mew ➔ *http://amzn.to/2f623mU*

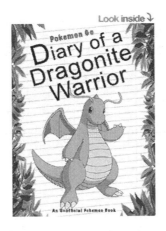

Diary of a Dragonite Warrior ➔ *http://amzn.to/2f7YngY*

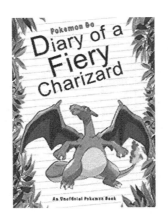

Diary of a Fiery Charizard ➔ *http://amzn.to/2e62lKa*

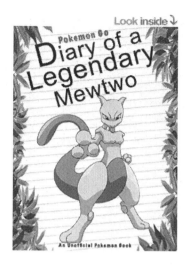

Diary of a Legendary Mewtwo ➔ *http://amzn.to/2dxdseJ*

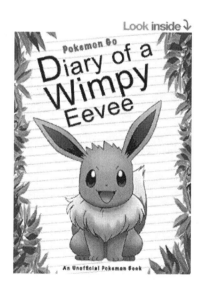

Diary of a Wimpy Eevee ➔ *http://amzn.to/2du9xQv*

Diary of a Farting Pikachu

Download Here: http://amzn.to/2dBSE4U

Diary of a Sleepy Snorlax

Download Here: http://amzn.to/2demOZW

Diary of a Fiery Charmander

Download Here: http://amzn.to/2bwYfHP

Diary of a Bulbasaur

Download Here: http://amzn.to/2bMm9Ps

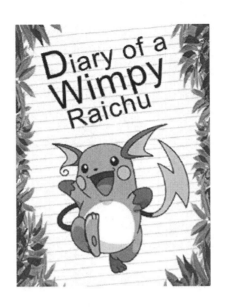

Diary of a Wimpy Raichu ➜ http://amzn.to/2cZfOz2

99 Amazing Facts that Will Blow Your Mind

Download Here: http://amzn.to/2bNeD4p

Diary of a Wimpy Pikachu 1 ==> http://amzn.to/2b0BfSC

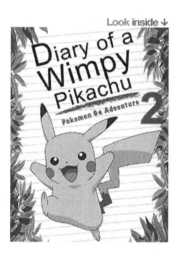

Diary of a Wimpy Pikachu 2 => http://amzn.to/2bHJW52

Diary of a Wimpy Pikachu 3 => http://amzn.to/2bSqa6L

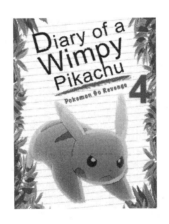

Diary of a Wimpy Pikachu 4 ➔ http://amzn.to/2cZgHb7

Diary of a Wimpy Pikachu 5 ➜ *http://amzn.to/2duuvNa*

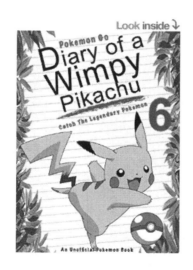

Diary of a Wimpy Pikachu 6 ➜ *http://amzn.to/2dbRkRX*

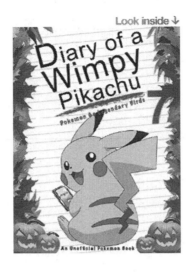

Diary of a Wimpy Pikachu 7 ➜ *http://amzn.to/2fpTUtV*

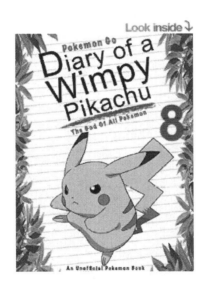

Diary of a Wimpy Pikachu 8 ➜ *http://amzn.to/2g0uzWW*

**SPECIAL EDITION → *Strange Origins of the Wimpy Pikachu
1 → http://amzn.to/2c3ANCd*

***SPECIAL EDITION → *Strange Origins of the Wimpy Pikachu
2 → http://amzn.to/2djsEae*

Want to learn the latest insider tips and secret guides on

Pokemon Go?

I would highly recommend these books by author Adrian King

Pokemon Go: Art Of War ➔ *http://amzn.to/2c40hAu*

Pokemon Go: The Legendary Leveling Guide

Download Here: http://amzn.to/2brAxhm

If you like reading this, you might like this "Diary Of A Wimpy Super Mario" series too

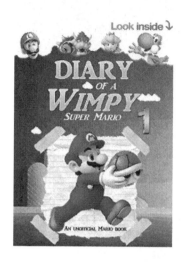

Get it here ➜ *http://amzn.to/2ejL6nT*

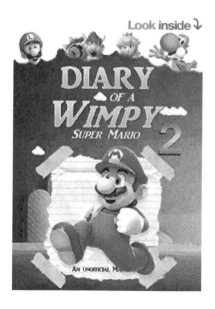

Get it here ➜ *http://amzn.to/2dFWls4*

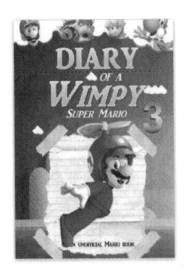

Get it here ➔ *http://amzn.to/2dqNNA5*

Made in the USA
San Bernardino, CA
16 December 2016